HOW TO BE A GOOD ROOMMATE, HOW TO BE A GOOD HOUSEGUEST, AND HOW TO BE A GRACIOUS HOST

CONTENTS

PART I: HOW TO BE A GOOD ROOMMATE

PART II: HOW TO BE A GOOD HOUSEGUEST

PART III: HOW TO BE A GRACIOUS HOST

www.nikki-allen.com
©2011

I

HOW TO BE A GOOD ROOMMATE

Chapter 1

A Few Things You Should Know Before Getting A Roommate

Have you and someone (whether you know them well or not) decided to "room" together? If so, here are a few tips before you venture into such a serious commitment. It is very possible that after you read this, you may have a change of heart.

Although having a roommate has its benefits, like cutting down expenses and companionship, it can still be a challenge. It is true what they say: "You never really know a person until you live with them". Always remember that!

Also know that there are legal responsibilities attached to having a roommate.

First of all, everyone that signs the lease is equally legally bound to uphold the lease agreement. If one person does not pay, it does not mean that the landlord is going to come after the negligent person only. Everyone that signed the agreement will be held responsible.

After all, your landlord only wants his money in full and on time, and could care less how the committed parties make that happen.

In terms of utilities, once you decide who is putting what into whose name, make sure you sign agreements on the arrangements that you work out. It does not matter that you have been best friends since diapers. All of that goes out of the window when dealing with money and possessions. You must now be accountable and responsible.

Chapter 2

A Few Rules To Keep The Peace

Well since you have decided that you actually want to have a roommate, here are some instructions that may help you keep a lot of the drama down.

Always have your own. The best scenario to avoid possible issues is to simply have what you want and need on hand, so that you are not relying on your roommate's "stuff".

Well again, in some cases you are close or best friends and you are used to going over each other's houses and sharing and taking. It was never a problem in the past, but it could become one now.

The fact is, you are now under one roof and whether you know your roommate well or not, their world probably does not revolve around you. Therefore, you cannot help yourself to their belongings. You cannot go into their closet or bathroom or any of their personal space and take things without their consent. Yes, I said personal space. Everyone is entitled to it...even married people. That's another book. Anyway, the main thing here is **NEVER TAKE OR USE _ANYTHING_ WITHOUT ASKING!!!!**

I will also add that if you do borrow something from your roommate, you need to return it in a reasonable amount of time or by the agreed date, in the same condition in which you borrowed it. You are responsible for any damage incurred to the property while in your possession.

To the person that is allowing their "stuff" to be "checked out", be clear on when they are to return it. Depending on what the item is or how valuable it is to you, it may be necessary to get that in writing as well.

Establish ground rules from the beginning! I understand that you just moved into your new place and you are excited, and have a lot of unpacking to do, but the novelty does wear off at some point, so it is better to take the time now to establish the rules.

Remember the night you and your roommate moved in and after dinner you did the dishes and your roommate took out the trash? Then, over the next week or so that was the routine until you realized that you did not want to be the designated dish washer, so you stopped but the attitude from your roommate began.

The problem here is you both are now operating from assumptions. Since they did "it" last time, they will do "it" from now on. There is an assumption that since they took out the trash and you did the dishes that it is to be like that forever. Not true!

Another wrong assumption is that since you too are paying rent that it is okay to invite friends over or have parties any time you want. Also, not true! Before you sign the lease agreement, you need to work out amongst yourselves your likes and dislikes, your differences, especially those of you who think you know the person you are moving in with. Once the ground rules are established, you need to put them in writing.

Here are a few things to consider in your agreement:

- Who does what chores?
- Who gets the bigger room and why?
- When to have friends over and how long can they stay?
- What about overnight guests? To have or not to have.
- Who takes or mails the rent to the office each month?
- Are you going to share phone lines?

Trust me! It may not seem like a big deal now, but at some point it very well could be.

What are the expectations of this relationship? What relationship? You know, "this is my buddy", "I've known him/her for years", "I'm doing this as a favor", or "we just met" relationship. So now, what is the expectation?

Because you are an introvert, are you expecting them to be like you or conform to your ways? Just because you go to bed at eight o'clock at night, do you expect your roommate to do the same? Does the house have to be completely quiet at a certain time? Are there phone hours, visiting hours, music hours, study hours? Those are just a few issues that I have seen or heard arise amongst roommates. You and your roommate need to have a discussion about these possible situations because you might find out that you may clash from the beginning.

Is everything fifty/fifty? In my experience, it is much easier if it is. However, sometimes equality is unavoidable so therefore modifications must be made to even the score.

For instance, you may choose a place that has a master bedroom and a regular bedroom. You must decide who gets which room and why. Once that is established, the person with the smaller room should either; **a)** be accommodated with another part of the house to balance out the space they do not have, or; **b)** pay less rent since they will not have an equal amount of space.

In terms of utilities, that should also be split down the middle. Nevertheless, be mindful of how much water, gas, electricity, etc. you use. Do not go overboard just because someone has to share the cost. As a matter of fact, time limits on showers and rules about leaving lights on is a great way to keep the peace when it come to paying for utility bills.

Also, once it is determined whose name the bill is established in, that person is responsible for paying that bill on time, regardless of what side arrangements you make, so setting payment schedules between you is a good idea.

Be respectful towards one another.
Although you may be paying half or a portion of the rent, always get clearance when it involves your common space, i.e. bathroom, kitchen, living and dining area.

It also may be good to designate "space" time, i.e. study time, company time, TV time, alone time, whatever time you need, especially in the common areas.

If you see your roommate engaging in a quiet moment like taking a nap, please do not come in and blast the TV or radio, or talk loud just because you pay a portion of the rent. Remember, so do they. Therefore give them the same courtesy that you expect and do it with a cheerful heart, no pouting or rolling your eyes or stomping.

I also want to strongly stress once again, to respect each other's personal space. Do not take anything that is not yours, I do not care how minute it may seem to you. Do not assume that your roommate is "cool" with it, even if they say "anytime", because the one time you take whatever it is, may be the one time they need that one thing. Hence, an argument ensues. Something we want to desperately avoid.

Chapter 3

Cover Yourself (Legally)

This is the part that is usually pretty touchy, but it is very necessary. When embarking upon any new relationship, you typically do not go in expecting things to turn into a nightmare. In fact, it is usually the opposite. You enter into this new relationship believing that things will be absolutely wonderful, as you should, but every now and then there are problems that need to be sorted out fairly and objectively. This is when contracts come into play.

PUT ALL AGREEMENTS IN WRITING – NO EXCEPTIONS! It can be uncomfortable, but once it is settled on paper, you will sleep easier knowing that there is nothing unknown, no surprises. Also, make sure that both of you sign the contract.

NO CASH! There is nothing more disturbing than watching court TV shows where the judge asks for proof that they paid and they say, "Your honor, I paid them in cash". You now have no proof and are relying on someone that you are in a dispute with to tell the truth. Sometimes they do, and sometimes they don't, but DO NOT put yourself in that predicament.

ALWAYS MAKE PAYMENTS WITH CHECKS OR MONEY ORDERS AND ALWAYS KEEP THE RECEIPT FOR YOUR RECORDS!!! Yes, it does require you to do some minor bookkeeping and exercise your organizational skills, but more importantly you are being responsible for you.

Remember, whichever bill is in your name, it is YOUR responsibility to pay it in full and on time. Make sure that you do even if your roommate fails to pay their portion. Failure to pay on your part will result in damaging your credit, not theirs. Again, receipts are crucial here in case you have to take your roommate to court to get reimbursed.

WHAT IF YOU FIND THAT YOUR ROOMMATE IS NOT COMPATIBLE AFTERALL? Unfortunately, that can be a reality as well. You sat down and hashed everything out, followed all of the steps and obeyed the rules, but for some reason there is no chemistry and you keep clashing. If you are still bound in a lease with one another, the best and easiest thing to do is to stay out of each other's way until the lease is up.

However, there can be the roommate from hell which makes your living space inhabitable. In this case one of you has to move. A couple of examples that could constitute that situation are;

A) Your roommate has an addiction to drugs or alcohol or something of that nature and you do not want to be in that environment.

B) They are bringing certain elements into your residence in which may not only be uncomfortable, but harmful.

C) Your roommate is not adhering to the agreements in which you both have signed.

If at all possible or when needed, take pictures, video record or whatever proof you can gather.

Now, I know I said that one of you has to move, but legally it is not that simple. I am not an attorney so I cannot give you any legal advice; therefore please seek counsel as to how to break your lease agreement.

Chapter 4

Common Sense...Not So Common

This may sound remedial and I am definitely not trying to insult your intelligence, but common sense is not as common as you think. Sometimes we just need a reminder, so here it is: please try and find someone compatible. If you are loud and like to party, find someone more like you. Even if you want your roommate to be your best friend and he/she is the exact opposite of you, rooming with them can potentially make them your enemy. If you want other friends over all the time and your roommate likes it completely quiet, this is a setup for disaster unless you both intend to compromise a great deal.

Unless you are in college living in a dorm, in which your choices may be limited, do not jump in too quickly with someone you do not know. If you are forced into a situation like living in a dorm, get to know that person as much as possible first, if you can. Find out their likes, dislikes, habits and anything else that is of concern to you, and remember, you will have to compromise. However, a lot of the basic rules previously mentioned still apply.

II

HOW TO BE A GOOD HOUSEGUEST

Chapter 5

Know The Difference:
Houseguest or Roommate?

People often get this wrong and it creates a wealth of problems. First of all, there are two types of houseguests. There are those that are visiting in which there is a "completion" date. No further time needed, but remember, you must mind your manners.

The other type of houseguest is the one who needs a place to stay due to certain circumstances and unsure of a "completion" date. Not only do you have to mind your manners, but understand that you are NOT a roommate.

YOU ARE ONLY A ROOMMATE IF YOU HAVE SIGNED A LEASE OR SOME SORT OF TENANT AGREEMENT WITH THE LEASING OFFICE, POTENTIAL ROOMMATE OR OWNER.

If your signature is not on any document that states that you are a tenant, than you are a houseguest. It does not matter that you are paying some of the bills or rent. If you are not legally bound to that property, then you are only visiting. That brings me to my next point.

Chapter 6

How Long Can/Should You Stay?

This can sometimes be a difficult question to answer depending on the situation. You may have found yourself in a quandary due to the downward spiral of our economy. Perhaps you have lost your home and found someone who is willing to take you in, but you are not sure how long this circumstance will last.

On the other hand, you could just be in a transitional state and can provide a definite timeline in which you need this temporary housing. In either case, as grateful as you are, know that your host is extending a courtesy to you and that you must be careful not to take advantage of them.

Do not wear out your welcome. If your host is generous enough not to tell you when you must leave, that does not mean that you can stay forever.

If you are unsure how long your current situation will last, at least set a reasonable time frame in which you plan to leave and discuss this with your host. They will truly appreciate that. In addition, stick with the timeline you set. That means diligently seek other options in order to keep your arrangement, whether it be to move in with someone else or be on your feet enough to move out. Keep your host informed of your progress. Yes, you must check in. If your host feels unappreciated or used in any way, you have set yourself up for a possible eviction.

Do not keep asking for extensions.
Depending on the situation one or two extensions may be tolerated, but no more than that. Also, do not ask for more than two weeks within that extension. You will begin to stink like dead fish. You may also begin to notice that your host is not as chipper as in the beginning.

Make your presence _UN_known. STAY OUT OF THE WAY! Remember, your host is trying to help you out, so be assertive in trying to make your stay a quick and unnoticeable one. There is nothing worse for a host who has worked hard to maintain their place, to come in and see you "chillin'", i.e. watching TV all the time or lying across the sofa, etc. Best scenario, get up early and be out of the house looking for a job or apartment or whatever you need.

Take out the trash or water the plants. Let your host see that you are productive and appreciate them. They are already paying extra on gas, electricity, etc. by you being there. Cut their expenses down as much as possible, even if you are paying them something. No one likes to see an increase in their bills.

Have your own cell phone, your own food, laundry detergent, soap, toothpaste, and so forth. Make sure you keep your area clean. They owe you nothing, but you owe it to them to show that you are making an effort.

Understand what is expected of you. If your host requires certain things from you like rules or terms, make sure that you comply. Do not enter into an agreement out of desperation if you truly do not agree because at some point this can get you put out. If you do not like what they are asking it is best for you to find somewhere else to go, or humbly ask for a compromise.

Also, ask what you can do for them and do it. Surprise them and make a meal, or bring a meal. Go the extra mile.

This is not your house. Bring as little as possible, only the bare necessities. Do not go in trying to redecorate or change the way they like their place. For example, if they do not like the drapes open, do not open them. If they like the house quiet and dark after a certain hour, be quiet and turn off the light. Yes, you are walking on eggshells, which should be more incentive for you to hurry and move on.

Have a back-up plan (Plan B). Everything may be going well, so you think, but your host wants you gone. It happens. Be prepared. Have an alternative plan. Do not be so dependent upon them.

Communicate. Keep your host abreast of your progress. Again, you must check in. If you do not and your host feels like you have been mooching, that is a quick way to get thrown out or cause unnecessary friction. This is especially key when staying with relatives or extremely close friends.

I know it may seem like you are doing a lot of butt-kissing (forgive the term), but humble yourself because they are doing you a tremendous favor. You are dependent upon them, so show your gratitude. You should want to go the extra mile.

Chapter 7

Your Host Wants You Out – Now!

Unfortunately, it does happen for whatever reason, but what should you do? What if you have nowhere else to go?

If your host is angry or mad, give them some space to let them cool down. You may have to leave the house or just go and start packing. Once you feel they are in a reasonable state of mind, try and find out what the problem is. Do not argue with them. It could very well be a misunderstanding that can be worked out for your good.

However, note that once you have been asked to leave the first time, something negative has been set in motion, whether consciously or unconsciously. So, although they may let you stay, there may be some tension. Also, they may be less enthusiastic about helping you and the next time an issue arises, they may want you gone and provide no explanation nor leave room for reasoning, even if it is not your fault. Have Plan B ready.

If unfortunately, there is no reasoning with them, **YOU MUST GO**. Plan B should take effect immediately, whether it is sleeping in your car, at a shelter, in a motel, or a friend's house for a night. Those are all much better options than a park bench, but sometimes that could be an unfortunate option as well.

ALWAYS BE PREPARED FOR THE MOVE!

Leave only with **your** belongings. No retaliation!

III

HOW TO BE A GRACIOUS HOST

Chapter 8

Hints For The Host

Before you extend your kindness and generosity, understand what you are entering into and what to expect.

First of all, make sure you establish a time limit. Before you commit to sharing your home, find out how long this possible inconvenience will last. Yes, an inconvenience (sorry guests).

It is an inconvenience when you are rearranging your lifestyle to help someone out. That does not mean that you do not want to do it, nor does it mean you will do it with an ungrateful heart, but you are extending yourself which is a wonderful thing.

Back to the time limit, be clear and up front about it. Let them know that you are prepared to extend yourself for that amount of time only. If your guest has a timeline and you are okay with it, be firm in making them commit to it. It is not a bad idea to put all of this in writing in case one of you suffers mild amnesia.

Stick to your end of the bargain. I understand that this is your house but integrity goes a long way. You never know when you may be in your guest's predicament. Nevertheless, there are some exceptions. If your guest is totally out of line with what you have agreed to or completely disrespectful, then by all means, exercise your right to put them out.

Try not to compromise too much or too often. You are only setting yourself up to be used, not intentionally, but we as human beings like to stretch everything as far as we can, including someone's generosity. This is not in every case, because your guest may really NEED you to bend, but judge the situation lovingly and according to how much you REALLY can and are willing to bend.

Chapter 9

My Guest(s) Is Related To Me

Another touchy part. How do you handle relatives? You feel obligated to help and so you do, without any rules, terms, etc. You have just set yourself up to be frustrated and stressed out, and maybe not wanting to go to your own home.

My advice is to of course follow the same instructions as before by putting things in writing, as uncomfortable as that may seem. Yet, it will let your relative know that you mean business and they will respect your space and your wishes. Also, by putting things in writing, and should this venture turn left and other family members want to get involved, you at least have proof of the breach.

What if your guest(s) is mom and/or dad? Well, remember when they used to tell you, "My house, my rules"? The same applies, especially if you are married. Parents need to comply with your requests as well; however, you cannot always be as rigid. Remember the saying, "I brought you in this world..."? If you can finish that statement, you have my point.

THIS DOES NOT APPLY TO ELDERLY PARENTS OR ANY RELATIVE HAVING SPECIAL NEEDS.

Chapter 10

A Gracious Host

When you agree to allow someone to stay with you, please be gracious. That person is usually in need and their esteem may be low, so the last thing they need you to be is a nag.

Be fair. Be rational. Be patient. This may prove difficult at times, but you did allow them to move into your home for whatever reason. If it seems that they are not trying to help themselves, talk to them. Maybe they really are and their efforts are not being made known. Or maybe their efforts do not look like what you think they should look like. Or perhaps they are incapacitated due to depression in regards to their situation. Communication is always key.

Speaking of keys, try to avoid giving them keys to your house. Your guest should make preparations to go and come when it is convenient for you. Keys imply residency, and are sometimes hard to get back.

If at all possible, never put anyone out on the street. If you truly cannot take them anymore, try and give them at least three days. You made the commitment to help, stick to it. Life has a way of rewarding you. Still, there are some exceptions:

- Stealing from you
- Continually using things that you have asked them not to
- Going into parts of the house or your possessions in which you have deemed restricted
- Being verbally or physically abusive
- Chronic laziness
- Continually disregarding any of your requests
- Any form of utter disrespect, i.e. slamming doors, arguing, etc.
- Creating a harmful or uncomfortable environment

If you have other bullet points please include them.

Often times it may seem really hard or uncomfortable to make an agreement, so get creative with it. Create a voucher with an expiration date, terms and conditions. This way, it softens the blow of telling them when they need to be out, and what is expected while they are in your domain. Make sure they sign it, and that way everyone is on the same page.

Chapter 11

Final Words

I hope this book helps you as you enter into the world of cohabitation in whatever fashion you choose. This is just a little nugget to help make it easier. I personally have been in each position so I understand clearly how each party feels.

Always try to treat people the way you want to be treated.

To those of you temporarily living with someone, I hope that you find your own place soon and remember to pay it forward.

To those of you who open up your homes, "Thank You"!

Finally, to those of you who are roommates, "Good Luck"!